MY SISTER'S KEYPER

A Workbook for Moms to Help Their Child with Special Needs Thrive

BY ERICA E. RYDER

The events and conversations in this book have been set down to the best of the author's ability.

First paperback edition October 2020

ISBN 978-1-7359670-2-8 (paperback)

ISBN 978-1-7359670-1-1 (ebook)

https://eveconnection.com

Table of Contents

Acknowledgements 3

Foreword 5

Infant Years 7

Toddler Years 11

Pre-School Years..15

Elementary School Years..19

Middle School Years 27

High School Years...33

The Next Chapter and Beyond...37

Glossary of Terms 41

Acknowledgements

As I sit back in my chaise lounge, close my eyes, and think about finally finishing my book, I smile. I smile thinking about this great accomplishment and the many people that encouraged me along this journey. My heart is overwhelmed with love, gratitude and thankfulness. I give God all glory!

I thank my Mom and Dad for giving me life. My Mom, Oprah Hodge, taught me to never give up, always speak up, and never say what I can't do. My Dad, Moses Hodge, (God rest his soul) instilled in me a solid work ethic and a curiosity for adventure. I am appreciative to my late husband, Isaac, that we brought our beautiful daughters into this world. I thank Taryn and Maya as my inspirations to write this book and share parts of our lives to help others.

To my supportive siblings; Ronnie, who affectionately called me Tank when I was younger because he said I was sturdy and low to the ground, for reminding me throughout my adult life that I am, "one strong Sistah". Paula, who freely lends advice and is the nucleus of our family. Jason, who I consider my personal better business bureau who always has my back. Tammy, my twin six years apart, the other half of our committee of two, the one who can finish my sentences and brings me to tears in gut-wrenching laughter almost every time we talk.

A heart-felt thanks to Taryn's loving Godparents affectionately known as Auntie "B" and Uncle Reggie (peacefully resting) for consistently showering our family with godly wisdom, guidance, and support. I am beyond grateful for the following amazing women, My Sister Girlfriends, that make up my care circle of support and lifelong friendships: Simone, Yvonne, Lori, Sheila, Crystal, Ennelle, Doris, Rhonda, April, Sonja, Amanda and Cheryl. I want to thank my coworkers that were my accountability partners to make sure that I was staying on track with writing this book. I am grateful for all of those that have prayed for me, encouraged me and reminded me that someone needed to hear my story.

I finally want to thank my friend, Allegra, who has been my coach, confidant, sounding board, and therapist; the person that has challenged me beyond my wildest dreams to think bigger and pushed me way past my own boundaries, even outside of this book. The best is still yet to come!

Foreword

This book is lovingly dedicated to my two heartbeats, Taryn Sydney and Maya Joy.

My Sister's Keyper was inspired and conceived in July 2015. Just as I was given the vision, I also was given the following scripture: "And do not forget to do good and to share with others, for with such sacrifices God is pleased." (Hebrew 13:16)

In Genesis 4:9 when the Lord asked Cain, where was his brother Abel, he replied, "Am I my brother's keeper?" Even though God knew Cain's wrongdoing towards his brother, Cain responded in a sharp tone as if to say, "Am I supposed to be watching over my little brother?" My personal response is, "Yes"!

Most of the information in this workbook is based on the things I have learned because of navigating and advocating for our oldest daughter, Taryn, as a young lady who is Intellectually and Developmentally Disabled, aka, she has special needs. However, the title of the book is a loving reflection of our younger daughter Maya, who is five years younger than her sister and is truly the best little-big sister anyone could have!

Keyper is a play on words that will allow this workbook to be used as a key to unlock the door to a great amount of practical information that I have learned from being Taryn's Mom. My resume was the only one selected for this job. It is a true blessing and an honor that I am trusted to take care of and raise her.

When I thought I had mastered being a Mom of an infant with special needs, she became a toddler. When I thought I had mastered toddlerhood, she started pre-school. When I got pre-school down pat, she went to elementary school. This story continued from middle school and on into high school. Then I hit a realization wall in 2015! Next year...Taryn would be graduating from high school! OMG!

I remember having a conversation with God one day and saying, "She is really going to be getting out of school very soon! Now what? I could not have learned all that I have over these years about navigating and mastering the special needs landscape only for our family? We are now coming to the end of this chapter." I felt like I was overflowing with a wealth of knowledge swirling around in my head and in my heart...and this was now the end of the road. Then it was impressed upon my heart, "it's not!" Right then I knew I had so much to share and others needed to hear it.

"And do not forget to do good and to share with others, for with such sacrifices God is pleased."

Infant Years

Being the brand-new Mother of an infant that has different needs than what you anticipated while pregnant is overwhelming. You may have read books like, "What to Expect When You're Expecting" or looked through every baby magazine available while waiting in the reception area of your OB/GYN visits. You may have also received advice or stories shared with you from family members or friends that already had babies. You may have daydreamed about all the fun and cute things you were going to do with your baby while you were on maternity leave. You now know your situation will be different.

What you had planned out in your mind and what your new reality actually is, seem worlds apart! Your child was born with a certain condition, complication or set-back that has now shaped your life in a way that was not imagined.

What do you do? You live.

You learn. You move forward.

REFLECTION

Logically I knew that the doctors, nurses, and technicians in the Neonatal Intensive Care Unit (NICU) were trying to keep our daughter alive. Taryn was born at 27 weeks gestation, but she was the size of a 24-week baby due to the excess fluid I was carrying due to having severe pre-eclampsia. She weighed 1 pound, 8 ½ ounces and was 12 inches long. She could fit in the palm of her father's hand.

At times I felt so helpless watching her being poked and prodded to get an ounce of blood from wherever she had a viable vein for testing. During her first twelve weeks of life in the hospital she had six blood transfusions and two spinal taps.

On one of my daily visits I walked right by another child's incubator that was in the space where our daughter was the day before. It was not uncommon for space to be made for a new incoming baby. As I searched the room, I did not readily find her, so I circled back around to the incubator of the other child. To my horror, the incubator I had passed was actually my daughter's! Sometime during the previous night, they had to draw blood from her tiny body, but evidently the only viable vein they could find was in her head; they had shaved a patch of her beautiful, dark, silky hair to do so. All I could do was cry. After crying for a while, feeling genuinely hurt and insulted that they had shaved her patch of hair, I got a tissue, dried my tears and pulled my emotions together. I soberly reminded myself that they had to do that to help keep her alive; the job of the Neonatal Intensive Care Unit (NICU) medical professionals was to keep our child alive....by any means necessary!

KEYS

- Breathe! – Close your eyes, take deep cleansing breaths, and think of a time while you were pregnant that made you smile. Show gratitude for being able to conceive and have a child. That is a miracle!

- Ask the doctors and nurses lots of questions about any procedures, medications, tests and things to expect with your child. This will give you a good understanding of the condition you and your child are facing.

- Allow yourself to feel every emotion that comes. It is ok to cry, be angry, sad, disappointed, scared, and/or feel that your body betrayed you and any other emotion you experience. It is natural and all part of the healing process.

- Be present. Do not be in denial. Your precious infant needs you fighting for them. You are the only one that was chosen to be their Mother. You can do this!

- If your child must stay in the hospital for a longer period, try to go home and get a few good nights of rest in your own bed. The hospital staff are the best baby-sitters you could possibly have.

- Consider having a journal to write down all your thoughts and questions as well as dates and times of different milestones for your child.

- Allow other people to help you. Let them cook you meals, do some housework, run errands or anything else that is helpful for you and your family.

SELF-CARE

One of the most important things you can do while you are walking through this new journey with your infant is to make sure you are taking care of yourself. If you do not take time for yourself, you will not be able to effectively take care of others.

- If you are released from the hospital before your baby:
  - Use this time to be home to get some sleep. Your body needs to recover and heal. You just had a baby.
  - Use this time to get your baby's nursery ready or to put the final finishing touches to it.

- Sit in the nursery or room your infant will be coming home to. Daydream and imagine ...see them in your arms. It will become a reality before you know it.
- You may want to stay at the hospital every waking moment with your baby, but you should set a schedule of how many hours a day to be there.
- Follow your doctor's instructions about your own physical, mental and emotional healing.

- When both you and your baby are home:

  - In this season, grab a little time for yourself. Use your bathroom as your own personal sanctuary, whether it is for five minutes or for ten minutes.
  - Try taking a bath or shower by candlelight to have some quiet, brief "away" time.
  - If you feel the need to have your baby nearby, place them in their car seat or infant carrier and place them right outside the bathroom door .
  - Take a nap when your baby is napping. Do not always feel obligated to do house cleaning or other household chores while your baby is napping. You don't have to do that! Enlist the help of others in your household to share with the chores, whether it is your spouse/significant other or other older siblings to help.
  - Have a family member, neighbor or friend come by to watch the baby for an hour so you can take a nap.

NEXT STEPS

1. Write down all your child's diagnoses:

_____

_____

_____

2. Write down the questions you have regarding your child's condition and diagnosis:

_____

_____

_____

3. Write down the answers you have received so far:

_____

_____

_____

4. Search the internet and read articles from trusted resources* to increase your knowledge of your child's condition so you can help them...and you. List the names of some of the articles you have read:

_____

_____

_____

5. Join a targeted parental support group. Listen and participate in the discussions. What is something that was shared by another parent that was helpful to you?

_____

_____

_____

6. Talk to other moms of children with similar special needs because they really understand what you're going through. You'll be great support for each other. Write this mom's name here.

_____

_____

_____

_____

Trusted sources: March of Dimes, Mayo Clinic, Google Local and Governmental Agencies.

Toddler Years

The toddler years are full of feelings of gratitude, stress, and wonder; thankful that your child is alive, but thinking about how to manage through this new world of doctor's visits, specialists, and therapists. At some point you must come to terms with knowing that the various milestones for your special child are going to be different than other-abled children. The books that you read while you were pregnant did not focus on being the parent of a child with special needs. Where was that section even in the bookstores? You now begin the next part of your journey down a different road.

You realize you start to become a master juggler and manager of many things. In addition to regular pediatrician visits you may also now be taking your child to specialist visits. There also could be in-home our outpatient physical, speech and occupational therapy services your child is receiving. Coupling this with working inside or outside of the home, having a spouse, partner or being a single Mom, cooking, cleaning and everything else in between, can leave you feeling quite overwhelmed.

Give yourself some slack and grace. Be flexible. It's OK if everything does not always go as you might have planned. This is where self-care is so important.

REFLECTION

It was the July 4th holiday, so we were sleeping in late because we did not have to go to work. We did not have to get up at the crack of dawn to prepare for our long commutes and drop off a child at daycare in the midst. Isaac would travel almost two hours door to door heading south to Philadelphia via car and then train, while I traveled for about an hour and fifteen minutes in the opposite direction.

Taryn came waddling into our room and with a little boost, she climbed up in our bed and laid between us. We all fell back to sleep. At some point I started to wake up from my deep sleep to a very faint but rhythmic movement in the small of my back. I scooted a little towards the edge of the bed to escape this contact. Even after moving, after a few minutes, I could still feel a light vibration through the mattress. When I rolled over to see what was going on, Taryn's eyes were rolled up towards the ceiling. Our three-year-old daughter was having her first full blown seizure.

After being transported to the emergency room of the medical center and spending a few days being observed, Taryn was diagnosed with the seizure disorder, Epilepsy – "a central nervous system (neurological) disorder in which brain activity becomes abnormal, causing seizures or periods of unusual behavior, sensations, and sometimes loss of awareness". (Mayoclinic.org)

To equip myself the best way I knew how in order to understand Taryn's condition and how to help her, I read every piece of material I could to understand about seizures/epilepsy. I immersed myself in learning. I learned about the different types of seizures, what caused or triggered them, the effects they had on her brain, what to do when she had one and how to train family members and friends what to do in the event she had one while in their care. Taryn started taking daily medicine in order to manage and minimize her seizure activity. I really did feel like I became Dr. Mom and a pharmacist all in one.

KEYS

- Listen to the advice of your toddler's trusted physician and specialists. If you trust them, then let them help you. Often, they may refer your toddler to a specialist that can help even further. Do not be afraid to ask them questions regarding a specific condition/diagnosis your child has.

- Read information the physicians and specialists give you about your child's condition/diagnosis, so you become knowledgeable. This will help you be aware and equipped to help them.

- As a parent, if you sense there is something different or that does not feel right about your child, immediately consult your child's pediatrician.

Note: All children are different and develop at their own pace, however, are you noticing any of the following examples of "something different"? Often your child's doctor will give you an information guide of some of the milestones they should be achieving at a certain age. This is a good measuring tool to use:

- Is there an extreme delay in your toddler walking?

- Is there an extreme delay in your toddler talking?

- Do you notice your toddler not responding to your voice or verbal queues that are appropriate for their age?

- Does your toddler have trouble with concentrating or doing age appropriate tasks?

- Do not be in denial! Do not be embarrassed! Do not let your mind or pride trick you into thinking "it" will go away, or they will "grow out of it."

- Get your child the necessary help, therapy, counselling, or medications they need to help them thrive.

- The sooner you get the needed assistance, the better your child's outcome will be in the long-run.

SELF-CARE

- Ask a family member or friend to babysit your toddler for an hour so you can get out of the house so you can have some quiet "me-time".

- Go for a walk, run a quick errand, have a kid-free chat with your husband/significant other or sit in the car and do absolutely nothing. Whatever you choose, it is time carved out for you.

- Trust me, if you start this practice now of honoring yourself by setting time aside to get a brief break from the responsibilities of caring for your child, it will become an easier practice as your child gets older. You will not have "Mom Guilt" for separating from your child for a few hours.

- Self-care also means realizing that you are not Super Mom and there are other things you can do to bring your stress level down. **Get others in your household to help, even your toddler.**

- You can have your toddler help pick up their toys, so you do not have to. Make a game of it. Toddlers love songs so sing the, "Clean Up" song together while they are picking up their toys and putting them away.

    - *"Clean up, clean up everybody everywhere, clean up, clean up everybody do their share."*

- If there are older siblings in the house, they can also help with things that are age-appropriate for them to do to help around the house.

Next Steps

1. Write down any concerns you currently have about your toddler so you can share with their pediatrician during their next checkup:

_____

_____

_____

2. If applicable, write down any type of therapy services your toddler is receiving such as speech, occupational, or physical therapy.

_____

_____

_____

3. What is something new you learned or observed while your child was having their therapy session?

_____

_____

_____

4. What are some things you can practice with your toddler between therapy sessions to help them?

_____

_____

_____

5. What are different activities your toddler likes to do?

_____

_____

_____

Pre-School Years

Time has really moved along. Depending upon where you live, the pre-school years may begin the entrance into the public-school system. This can be a very scary time for you as the parent and if you are not careful, you can cast this fear onto your child. You want to help them feel as safe and confident as possible with the changes that are happening. There will be registration and various testing that your child will undergo to assess their academic needs and potential class placement. There will be IQ testing, psychological evaluations, Individual Education Plans (IEPs) and the like. This is where you will need to continue to develop and grow your advocacy skills so you can continue to fight for what your child needs and is entitled to. Your advocacy for your child will make the difference between them *surviving* with special needs versus *thriving* with special needs.

What is advocacy? Advocacy is the act of

pleading for, supporting, or recommending;

active espousal (adoption) as of a cause

or principle. (Dictionary.com)

If your child's pre-school years begin at a daycare, make sure you have done your research and are comfortable the facility has trained professionals and the support to accommodate the special needs of your child. Ask to observe the classes a few times at various times of the day so you can get a good sense of how the daycare is run. You also want to see the professionals that are trained to work with children with development or intellectual disabilities in action.

REFLECTION

Our preschool journey started in North Brunswick, NJ at Judd Elementary School. Taryn's new school outfit was so cute. She had on a khaki skort, a green long-sleeved cotton shirt with little flowers on it, matching green bobby socks and black, buckled, strapped leather shoes.

The "short bus" picked our daughter up on the first day of school right in front of our townhouse. Once she was on the bus, my husband and I hopped in our car and followed the bus to the school. Once at the school, we parked our car in the far lot so she would not notice us. We got out and hid behind one of the larger buses and watched as her new teachers extended their hands and greeted her off the bus. She flashed her tiny smile, I shed a tear, but knew she would be just fine.

By this time, I had become very good at asking lots of questions of Taryn's doctors and the different therapists that worked with her to become as knowledgeable as I could, so I knew what to expect. I became equally good at asking for what I felt she needed as her Mother to help her and would not settle for anything less. **The professionals are great, but an in-tune Mom knows her child best.**

Her first self-contained pre-school class had eight students, one head teacher, one speech therapist and one occupational therapist. Additionally, because Taryn also has mild cerebral palsy, along with her depth-perception being compromised, she also had a personal aid to help her until she learned to safely maneuver around the class on her own.

KEYS

- Your child will start to get various tests performed on them to assess their cognitive, motor, emotional and physical skills. Ensure you receive copies of all of the results and request that the professionals sit down with you and explain what everything means.

- Do your research. Do your homework. Continue to equip yourself with knowledge. This will help you feel like you have some control over a condition or circumstance you have little control over.

- You may feel like the professionals have all the answers because they are trained and have letters behind their names. However, you are your child's Mother and are with them almost 24/7. That is why the professionals ask you questions during a doctor's visit or some other type of appointment. You are the one that helps them help your child. You and the professional are partners in helping your child thrive.

SELF-CARE

- Increase your bathroom sanctuary me-time so you can take a longer bath or shower by candlelight. Adding some aroma therapy (lavender and chamomile) will help you feel like you are at your own personal spa.

- If your little one needs to be near you, then set them safely outside of the closed bathroom door with all their favorite toys and books to keep them occupied while you are in the bathroom. Their little fingers might wiggle under the door, but you are still letting them know that Mommy is near, but Mommy needs to be by herself for a few minutes.

- You may also decide not to take a bath or shower but sit on the side of the tub or on the toilet to catch up reading a magazine article or a chapter in a book. The key is this time is yours. You are starting to build your child's understanding as well as that of your spouse/significant other, that you need this time for you. This time helps you to de-stress and regroup.

- If you have designated a different place for your me-time or your happy place, then go there.

NEXT STEPS

1. Write down how you are feeling right now.

_____

_____

_____

2. Write down something your child did today that made you smile.

_____

_____

_____

3. What is something new you learned today?

_____

_____

_____

4. Does your child have a favorite bedtime story they like you to read to them? Write down the title of that book. Enjoy the precious bonding time of you reading it to them.

_____

_____

_____

Elementary School Years

Testing, evaluations, Individual Education Plans (IEPs), goal setting, progress reports and meetings will become the norm as your child officially begins their journey through elementary school. If this is your first child to navigate through this new education system, you will quickly learn that it is very different from what you may be accustomed to. It is different from your regularly-abled child's experience and probably different from when you were in elementary school years ago. It is very different from what you may remember when you were in elementary school years ago.

In addition to the regular education classroom teacher, you may now have to interact with a whole host of other individuals based on your child's "area of eligibility" based on their medical diagnosis. There may also be the Special Education teacher, the Exceptional Children's (EC) teacher, Speech Therapist, Occupational Therapist, Physical Therapist, the Education Initiative Administrator, School Psychologists, the EC Facilitator and EC Coordinator. You will become familiar with your child's entire teaching team and come to understand that it truly does "take a teaching-village" to help educate your child. You are all partners now.

> *It is very important to understand and embrace your lifelong role as your child's advocate; you are their voice, their champion; the one who speaks up for them because they can't themselves.*

REFLECTION

I thought I had thoroughly done my homework before we arrived in North Carolina in July of 2002, but I was wrong. It was very frustrating to learn that our daughter's classification of "multiple handicapped" meant something totally different in New Jersey than it did in North Carolina. Also, the level of support we were accustomed to was vastly different.

"Multiple handicap" in New Jersey meant that she had multiple diagnoses; epilepsy, learning delay and cerebral palsy. Her daily teaching team in the class of eight students consisted of the regular education teacher, a speech therapist and her personal assistant to help her navigate through the classroom and school. She even had a special chair that helped with her posture and spatial awareness.

On the other hand, the classification of "multiple handicap" in North Carolina landed our daughter in a classroom of profoundly handicapped children; many who were in wheelchairs and nonverbal. This was our first test of advocacy in the elementary school setting to get her moved out of that class into a class that was more suited for her functional abilities. It took over a month to get her placement corrected. In the meantime, with her kind-hearted spirit, our daughter would often spend her day pushing her classmates around in their wheelchairs and being a helper to her less-mobile or abled classmates.

Our next biggest advocacy challenge was to get the exceptional children's classroom relocated from the trailer in the far side of the parking lot to inside the building. Yes, at the second elementary school she attended in NC, the special needs students were being taught in a trailer in the parking lot. We expressed extremely strongly at every meeting we had with the principal, Exceptional Children's Coordinator and all involved parties that if the goal was to, as had been stated often, make the special education students "feel a part" of the regular education students, then they had it all wrong! I would ask repeatedly, "then why in the world would you make these children that already feel different "schlep" across the parking lot and be isolated like outcasts?" (Schlep Definition: "Haul or carry something awkwardly" (verb) or "a tedious or difficult journey" (noun).

Needless to say, before too long, the room that was once the teacher's lounge that was across from the cafeteria was transformed into the exceptional children's classroom. Victory; I felt like David going up against Goliath by winning this battle. This reinforced my drive to always advocate for what was best for Taryn, no matter how long a process or system has been in place and how insurmountable things may look. The other thing that I am also reminded of is that when changes are made, it not only benefits Taryn, it benefits her fellow classmates and their families as well. We are really on this special journey together.

KEYS

- You know your child best and what they are capable of achieving. Challenge them to be the best according to their ability. Some days will be better than others. Be patient with them and yourself.

- Treat your relationship with your child's teaching team as a partnership. Communicate regularly to address any issues or concerns.

- Always take a pen and paper/notebook to all IEP (Individual Education Plan) meetings. Ask as many questions as you need until you feel everything was answered to your satisfaction and understanding.

- The IEP meetings can be intimidating because the teaching team usually outnumbers the one or two of you parents. You can opt to have a parent advocate come with you or have a trusted friend accompany you for support.

- If you feel like your child is not receiving all the services they need to thrive, you must speak up and have it documented in the IEP meeting notes. It is critical that everything is documented in the IEP. This is your child's official education plan that will follow them throughout the school year to note their progress. This also holds the teaching team accountable to helping your child achieve the set goals.

- Remember this, your child is entitled to a Free Appropriate Public Education in the United States. If the school cannot provide a certain needed service, then the district must supply it. If the district cannot supply it, then the State must provide it.

- If your child needs a particular service to help them learn in the public school setting, it is guaranteed by the Rehabilitation Act of 1973 and the Individuals with Disabilities Education Act.

- Read through the IEP carefully and make sure you agree with everything that was written **before signing it**. That is your right as a parent.

- Read through the entire copy of the ***"Handbook on Parent's Rights and Responsibilities in Special Education"*** for your state so you fully understand your rights and responsibilities as your child's parent advocate. This handbook should be supplied to you by the Special Education team from your child's school. It can also be located on your state's Board of Education and Department of Instruction website.

- Set a life goal for your child. Where do you see them in twenty years? What do you picture them doing or achieving by that time? **Use this future image of them as a guidepost as you move through the years.** Be honest with yourself. Be honest with them. Base this goal upon their abilities and potential. You know your child best.

SISTER'S KEYPER REFLECTION

Early one morning in October 2005 around 4:30am, Isaac and I woke up startled to the rapid pounding of a little fist on our bedroom door. As we sprang out of bed, ran to the door and opened it, no one was there, but we saw the girl's bedroom door was open and the light on. When we ran to their bedroom we found Taryn laying on the floor and Maya's little body hovered over her. Taryn was about 9 years old so that meant Maya was about 4 years old. Unfortunately, Taryn was having a full blown epiletic seizure. Maya was on the floor next to her sister, holding her one hand, and with her other hand, gently caressing her forehead, fearlessly and calmly telling her, "it's OK.....Sister....you're going to be OK!"

Our natural family cadence in these situations was Maya would alert us and run back to comfort her sister. I would usually arrive next with Isaac following closely behind. The majority of the time, the seizure would run its course in about 5-10 minutes and the episode would be done. Being totally drained, Taryn would then fall back asleep so her body could fully recover. Unfortunately, this was not one of those times. The episode lasted more than 10 minutes which prompted me to call the paramedics. We continued to lay hands on Taryn while Isaac prayed for healing over her body until the paramedics arrived. Once they arrived I would calmly answer every question they asked to assess Taryn's condition. But during this one particular episode Maya decided she would start telling the paramedics exactly what had just happened. The paramedics looked at her in disbelief; that this little person was literally telling them blow-by-blow what happened without any hesitation or fear.

Just by virtue of being her sister,
Maya had become Taryn's Guardian Angel.

KEYS

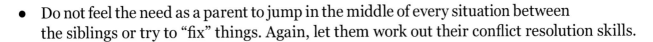

- The bond between siblings is strong. Recognize its strength! There are things between your children that parents will never know about or experience.

- Despite this strong sibling relationship, as a parent, do not put the responsibility of parenting your child with special needs on your other child(ren). That is your responsibility, not theirs.

- Do regular self-reflection. Make a daily/ weekly mental note to assess how you are doing to ensure the parenting responsibility lines are not blurred. You do not want your other child(ren) growing up possibly resenting being put in the position of having to be the "pseudo" parent.

- As a parent, you set the temperament and rules of your home. Let the siblings form and work out their own relationships, conflicts, etc., under the guidance of those rules.

- Do not feel the need as a parent to jump in the middle of every situation between the siblings or try to "fix" things. Again, let them work out their conflict resolution skills.

- Be mindful to regularly set meaningful one-on-one time aside for your other child(ren). Having a child with special needs that requires your constant attention can leave other siblings feeling left out or neglected (mentally, physically and emotionally). They may not readily say anything, but they may be feeling that way inside.

- Acknowledge and thank your other children regularly for all the things that they do to help their special needs sibling; the things you see, but more importantly, the things you never see.

SELF-CARE

- Remember to utilize your support system and care circle as needed to help you.

- Get yourself a manicure, pedicure or both.

- Get a babysitter and have dinner with your spouse, significant other or a friend.

- Go to the movies by yourself and enjoy the snacks you like without having to share with anyone (you're not supposed to talk in the movies anyhow!).

- Get a relaxing massage.

- Make that hair appointment you have been putting off.

- A little "budgeted" retail therapy may also do the trick. Buy an item you like or have been putting off just for you.

- Check your purse, wallet, drawers, etc. for gift cards you may have received. Use them on yourself (not the kids) before they expire.

- Indulge in your favorite "guilty pleasure" food from time to time...and don't share with anyone. Take the time to enjoy every morsel.

- Go to lunch or your favorite coffee shop alone.

NEXT STEPS

1. Close your eyes. Visualize what you see your child doing at age twenty. Write down what comes to your mind.

_____

_____

_____

2. Write down any questions you have or things you do not understand as a result of reading the Parent's Rights Handbook.

_____

_____

_____

3. Write down all the names of your child's teaching team as well as their titles and how to get in contact with them:

_____

_____

_____

4. If you have not done so already, get involved with your child's school. Join the PTSA, commit to volunteering as a class parent, help supply the class with snacks or chaperone a field trip. Write down what you will commit to do.

_____

_____

_____

5. If applicable, write down the names of your other child(ren). Next to each of their names, write down 3-5 adjectives that describe them. Also write down their dreams and aspirations, not yours for them.

_____

_____

_____

Middle School Years

Just when we finally figured out the ins and outs of effectively navigating through the elementary school maze of learning and advocating for our daughter, it was time to transition to middle school. We were just starting to get good at this and now it was time to move to a new level of learning and advocating.

The same principles and rhythms should be applied in middle school as in previous years. Stay involved by being in regular contact with your child's teaching team, being present at each IEP meeting and understanding your child's individual education needs. You need to know what they should be learning for them to grow and thrive.

Now that you have been in this type of parenting mode a while, it is time to expand your "Circle of Support". Your "Circle of Support" are those people in your life that have helped you along the way, big and small. Another way of understanding this particular concept is through the phrase you may have heard many times, "It takes a village to raise a child." Those people in your circle have been grandparents, sisters, brothers, babysitters, Pastors, teachers, friends, neighbors, counsellors, doctors, etc. They are the people in your everyday life that have helped you in some way. You cannot do this parenting work alone! It's impossible! You need help and it's OK to need and ask for help. This doesn't make you a bad parent or any less of a person. It just means you are human and are being wise.

Unless you are a parent of a child with special needs, it's hard to fully understand the ins and outs, the ups and downs, and how draining it can be physically, mentally, and emotionally. Those genuinely closest to you (and this is not necessarily a blood relative) will empathize and try their best to understand, so let them support you any way they can.

REFLECTION

One of our very first encounters at middle school was that our daughter was placed at the wrong school in the wrong exceptional children's focused program. It was like deja vu when we had first moved down to North Carolina. She was placed in a class that had more of a focus on children with autism. Even though two of her buddies that she absolutely adored and hung out with in the same class in elementary school were in that same class, she was not on the spectrum. She had different needs and needed to be placed in the correct setting to help her thrive best.

There was another factor that we were not pleased about, yet again. The special needs class was placed in a trailer that was near the back of the building. Again, it had a makeshift walkway that kind of connected it to the main building, however, it was still a trailer!

Although the teacher did her best to accommodate our daughter's needs, we contacted the necessary personnel in the Exceptional Children's department at the Board of Education to start the process to get her placed in a more suitable setting. Unfortunately, she had to spend her entire sixth grade year in the wrong school and setting, but was finally moved to the year-round middle school for seventh and eighth grade. That program better suited her learning style with different techniques to address her continued occupational and speech therapy needs, as well as how her brain took more time to process information. The teacher was absolutely wonderful! He was an awesome educator that cared deeply for the needs of each child in his class and the teaching assistant was just as amazing with her care, concern and commitment.

Even though Taryn spent her sixth grade year in the wrong class setting that catered more towards autistic learners, that experience reminded me of the following:

- Children are very resilient, oftentimes more than adults.

- Life does not always go as planned, but keep on pressing forward and keep on living.

- Stay focused on your goals and persevere.

- What doesn't hurt you makes you stronger.

- Keep on advocating!!!

- There is a lesson in everything.

Keys

- Don't be afraid to express any concerns you have regarding what your child is being taught or how they are being taught. You want to make sure they are progressing forward in a manner specific to their learning needs.

- Treat your relationship with your child's teaching team as a partnership. Communicate regularly to address any issues or concerns.

- Always take a pen and paper/notebook to all IEP meetings. Ask as many questions as you need to until you feel everything was answered to your satisfaction and understanding.

- Read through the IEP carefully and make sure you agree with everything that was written before signing it. That is your right as a parent.

- Repeat....read through the entire copy of the "Handbook on Parent's Rights and Responsibilities in Special Education" so you fully understand your rights and responsibilities as your child's parent advocate.

- Expand your circle of support. As your child is getting older this may now include:

  - Other parents
  - Church
  - Support groups
  - Friends

- Set expectations for your child to strive their hardest to reach their full potential. This is different for every child. As their parent, you should know what they are capable of doing and not doing. Lovingly push them to be the best them, they can be. If you set the bar high, they will look to achieve it. You are their biggest coach and cheerleader!

- Get them involved in social events and special camps to help build their confidence, to socially interact with others besides their immediate family. Some examples are:

  - Special Olympics
  - Classmates birthday or pool parties
  - Victory Junction Camp/Summer Camps
  - Dinner dates with friends

- Encourage and teach them a level of independence and responsibility that suits them and their abilities at their pace. This may include:

  - Doing chores around the house
  - Cleaning their own room
  - Sorting clothes for laundry
  - Putting up groceries

All of these are like building blocks to help your child thrive in the future. Continue to stack your experiences and gain knowledge on top of each other along this special parenting journey. There are not necessarily right or wrong ways to successfully parent a child with special needs, but there are many different and unique experiences. Every child is unique, but you must be active, present and willing to proactively seek out information to help them live the best, fullest and most productive life for them.

Side note: June 8, 2012 - this is the date that Taryn received her Certificate of Completion from middle school. She will be off to high school in the Fall where a new chapter will begin as we move closer to adulthood.

SELF-CARE

- Take care of yourself! This cannot be stressed enough! If you don't take care of you, who will? You do not want to experience continuous overload and burnout. It will happen if you don't manage it. Don't try to be a Super Mom.

  - Take time for you - what is that thing you used to do that you have not done in it feels like forever?
  - Read a chapter of a good book

- Take a walk
- Call a friend
- Set time to do an hour or two of your favorite hobby
- Go to the movies

- Get away - it is very important that at some point you get away, whether you are a single parent or a married couple. This is where your trusted circle of support/care is essential. You have to detach and regroup at times in order to keep your sanity. Some examples of getting away may be:

  - While your child is at school, you take off the day and do something specific for you. The teachers and the school are your care support for that day.
  - Have a night out. Call in that trusted friend, babysitter, grandparent, etc.
  - Take an overnight or weekend getaway.

- Get counselling - you are not crazy, even if it feels like that sometimes. Bottom line, this is hard, but you can do it! Utilize the services available to you through your job, church, support groups, etc.

NEXT STEPS

1. What activities or hobbies has your child shown an interest in? Write them down.

_____

_____

_____

2. Write down the ways you can help to cultivate that interest even more. For example, if they like to draw, buy them a notebook or sketch pad and some colored pencils.

_____

_____

_____

3. Write down the name of the high school your child will most likely be attending in a few years. No...it's not too early to do this because this time will go by incredibly fast. That time will be here before you know it.

_____

_____

_____

4. Use your teaching support team to help you as you begin to start discussions about high school. Become familiar with the curriculum and programs offered that best suit your budding high schooler.

_____

_____

_____

High School Years

The idea that your child is now entering high school can be exciting and scary all at the same time. It's hard to believe that in a few short years they will complete their K-12 education journey. It is really going to happen! What has grown to be your norm of IEP meetings, counseling sessions, report cards, therapy sessions, etc., as you have known them will start to shift during these years.

Now, you will have more thoughts of what they will do after high school. Post high-school life will start to be a regular part of your discussions with your family and teaching team.

- Will they be ready and able to get a job?

- Do they want to go to college and if so, what college offers the right accommodations for your child to stretch and enhance their abilities?

- Will they still live at home with your or will they live in some type of supported community?

These might be just a few of the endless questions you will be seeking answers for.

REFLECTION

As with previous transition experiences to the next level of schooling, starting high school also began on shaky ground. The high school teacher that taught the Exceptional Children's class resigned at the end of the previous school year. Recruitment of a new teacher was supposedly taking place over the summer and the new teacher was to be in place at the beginning of the school year. We were assured during the open house night that everything was being worked out and the new teacher would be in place.

The school year began but no new Exceptional Children's teacher was in place. We kept being promised that the new teacher was coming. Meanwhile, a substitute teacher was put in the class to pretty much "class sit" and give out menial work assignments to keep the students occupied. One week turned into two weeks, two weeks turned into three weeks without a permanent teacher in place. The class was led by substitute teachers and teaching assistants for almost the first month of class. Needless to say, this was beyond unacceptable to us as Taryn's parents.

Meetings were held with the principal and numerous phone calls were placed and emails sent to the Durham Public School's downtown main office and the Exceptional Children's office expressing our intense displeasure. Our years of advocating for our daughter was brought to a new level and we were very well equipped to tackle this issue head on. We were not going to let up on the emails and phone calls to everyone that was in a position to make things happen. Finally, the new teacher was put in place and the students authentic learning could begin.

We continued to be very involved parents and did our very best to support the teacher, the teachers aid and the entire EC class. The class was like a small family of some really determined students. Within the class new friendships were made, old friendships rekindled and new life skills were being taught. By the middle of the school year we had built a great rapport with the teacher because of our sincere involvement.

It was before the start of one of our daughter's Individual Education Plan (IEP) meetings that the teacher sincerely thanked us for our diligence and consistent pushing at the beginning of the year to get him started as the new teacher. He also shared that there was some real bureaucracy going on with his old principal not wanting to release him from his position at his prior school. He said it became really messy. Unfortunately, this "messiness" was at the expense of children getting used to their new high school environment and learning, namely, our daughter.

> *One thing we always knew; when we were*
> *fighting for our daughter, we were also*
> *fighting for other students and their families*
> *as well. This was no solo act. This was fighting*
> *for a very special village of individuals.*

In the end, the past twenty years of this schooling season paid off. Our daughter confidently and courageously walked across the stage at the Duke Cameron Indoor Stadium on May 5, 2016 to receive her high school diploma!

KEYS

- Take a deep breath and smile! Acknowledge all of the hard work you put in to get to this point in the journey. Be proud! Celebrate!

- Trust your judgement with all the knowledge you learned over the years in advocating and being there for your child. You have become their expert.

- Understand that this is not the end of the road just because high school is ending. Your advocacy and assistance will take on a different form as they become young adults.

- Continue to work closely with your child's teaching team as you support one another in helping your child become more independent and move into adulthood.

- Utilize all resources that are available to help support your child. These may include:

  - Vocational Rehabilitation Services
  - Job Training Programs (ex.Project Search https://www.projectsearch.us/)
  - Organizations that support adult IDD communities (ex. Reality Ministries https://realityministriesinc.org/)
  - Some colleges make certain accommodations (ex.more time to test) for individuals with learning disabilities.

- **Special Note:** Truly evaluate if you and your child are ready to exit the public school system. In most states, a student can remain in high school up to the age of twenty-two (22). Think about what is beneficial to your child and your personal family circumstances. Some questions to ask yourself in making this decision:

  - Are they intellectually and emotionally ready?
  - Have I done my homework and put everything in place for their next chapter in life?
  - Will they go to college, a vocational school, a training program or work?
  - Have I set up all the support systems they will need since they will no longer be in school?
  - Where will they live?
  - What will they be doing during the day now that they are no longer in school?
  - Do they have transportation to get around?

- Evaluate where you and your child honestly are towards achieving their life goals that were set. Re-evaluate the goal and make any necessary adjustments.

SELF-CARE

- Continue to incorporate all of the previous examples of self-care into your daily living.

- Keep expanding and relying on your circle of support to help you through this new time of transition.

- Give yourself grace ahead of time. You will make mistakes and miss things, but you will definitely learn new things along the way because of these misses.

- Remember to incorporate daily exercise or movement to help manage your stress. Examples include walking, gardening, dancing while you are doing household chores, parking far away from stores to promote more walking, taking the steps instead of the elevator, etc.

- Try your best to prepare and eat healthy meals.

- Ensure you are keeping up with all of your annual medical exams and screenings.

- Strive to be the best form of you!

NEXT STEPS

1. List any of your current fears:

_____

_____

_____

2. Write down what you think is causing your fears:

_____

_____

_____

3. What are the plans you and your child have for what they will do after high school?

_____

_____

_____

4. List all activities, hobbies, organizations, etc. your child is participating in:

_____

_____

_____

5. Circle how prepared you feel you are for your child to graduate from high school and move on to the next chapter of their life:

   1   2   3   4   5   6   7   8   9   10

Not at All Prepared   Somewhat Prepared   Very Prepared

The Next Chapter and Beyond...

Each new day is filled with uncharted territory as you continue to learn how to co-navigate this special world for your young adult child after leaving high school. They are no longer in the protective world of the public-school system where you worked with a team of teachers and professionals throughout the years. They are now transitioning into the real world as a young adult and you need to learn daily how to try to find balance between advocating for them and when applicable, teaching them how to speak up for themselves. It's a new skill we have to learn as parents of a young adult with special needs, and it is not easy.

Sometimes you are trying to be a coach on the sidelines, but then all of a sudden you have to jump in the game because you see a decision being made or an action taken that may put your child at-risk in some way. You are in a constant teaching mode. It's really a fine line between knowing when to help and when to allow time for the learning process to take place.

This season requires a lot of patience and understanding that your role as a parent is changing and shifting. There are many questions that you need to answer and address. The list below is just some of the questions you may need to ask yourself. It is not a full list, but it's a good start.

REFLECTION

I have learned over the years to break down large, daunting tasks and projects into smaller pieces. This makes tackling them easier. This new season of learning to be more of a coach and slowly letting go of the apron strings is no different. There is a lot of information to deal with that cannot be ignored. It can be very intimidating and overwhelming. The truth of the matter is that if life goes in its normal order, I will leave this earth before my children. Therefore, while I am still here, I want to make sure, as much as possible, I put things in order and in place. One of the best investments I made was to consult with a Special Needs Attorney to make sure all of my affairs are in order and that my daughters will be well taken care of with the guidance of my loving family, friends and supportive community. With such planning comes a great sense of peace as my girls and I continue to live our lives to the fullest!

KEYS

- Have you sought out the professional help you need? These may include physicians, specialists, counsellors, therapists, vocational rehabilitation resources, job training programs, caregiver support groups, etc.,

  - One of the best ways to find out about help is to ask other parents or caregivers of special needs individuals, trusted friends, colleagues, neighbors, etc.

- Are you allowing your support circle to continue to help you?

  - Remember it's OK to ask for help. Continue to establish your support circle and use them when you need them. They are willing and happy to help.

- Is your child with special needs capable of making their own decisions?

  - Determine how much support your child still needs from you. Where you can substitute your help with another individual or agency, do it. It helps to foster independence for your young adult. An example of this would be if they work, instead of you taking them to work, teach them how and trust them to ride the supported bus/van system.

- Will they be able to live on their own or in a supported community away from you?

  - Determine if, at some point, they will be able to live on their own with your support or in a community-supported living arrangement.

- Do you need to become their guardian?

  - Remember that once your child with special needs turns 18 they are technically an adult and have the right to make their own decisions. They still may need your assistance in making decisions, but ultimately, they have the final say, unless you have full guardianship of them. Guardianship is a legal proceeding in which someone (usually a family member) asks the court to find that a person is unable to manage his or her affairs effectively because of a disability. A guardian steps in the shoes of the person with a disability and makes the decisions for them. Being a person's guardian takes away a great amount of your young adult's independence. Consider this very carefully.

- Do you need to have Power-of-Attorney over their finances, medical decisions?

  - An alternative to guardianship may be Durable Power of Attorney. This is when your child with special needs can make competent decisions about various situations. They enter into a power of attorney which legally names one particular person to make certain types of decisions on their behalf.

- Do you have a Will? If yes, is your Will up-to-date with your current desires?

  - Make sure you have a Will and that it is up to date. It is recommended that you consult with an attorney that has experience and specializes in special needs individuals. They can give you guidance on how to protect your assets as well as making sure your child's benefits and services are also protected.

- Do you have a Letter of Intent created? Is it updated?

  - A Letter of Intent is a document, usually written by a parent, that outlines the needs of your child for future caregivers, guardians or trustees. It's goal is to make sure they are cared for in a manner they are used to once the parent is no longer around. *See example of information to include at https://www.specialneedsalliance.org/blog/letter-of-intent-3*

- Is your loved one eligible for Social Security Benefits?

  - Since your child has special needs they may be eligible for Supplemental Social Security benefits. *See Part III - Listing of Impairments (Overview) at https://www.ssa.gov/ disability/professionals/bluebook/listing-impairments.htm*

- Are they eligible for Medicaid or Medicare?

  - Your child may be eligible for Medicare or Medicaid. *See NC Medicaid: Eligibility for Medicaid or Health Choice at https://medicaid.ncdhhs.gov/medicaid/get-started/ eligibility-medicaid-or-health-choice*

- Have you consulted with an attorney that specializes in Special Needs Trusts? Have you set one up?

  - A **special needs trust** is a **trust** tailored to a person with **special needs** that is designed to manage assets for that person's benefit while not compromising access to important government benefits.

- Do they plan on attending a trade school or college that provides accommodations?

  - Will your child attend any type of job training program or vocational school? Do they want to and are they capable of attending college? There are many colleges that will make accommodations to support the needs of your child while they are a student.

- Have you looked into the various programs and resources available (examples: Bus transportation, discount services to local YMCA, etc.)

  - Research all of the various programs and services that your town or county may have to help support you and your child.

FINAL REFLECTION

After giving birth to Taryn I was in the hospital a total of nine days before being released to continue my recovery at home. I had to leave my baby in the hospital as she continued her fight to live. Logistically, my head understood but my heart was crushed. She stayed in the hospital the first three months of her life before she was able to come home just before Thanksgiving. She was our little Butterball turkey that had fought hard to gain the weight she needed to come home. She weighed 1 lbs 8 ½ ounces when she was born and weighed 4 lbs 2 ounces the night we brought her home from the hospital.

A few days after giving birth I remember having one really tough day. My system was really out of whack and my vital signs were all over the place. My body was still reacting to the trauma it had gone through giving birth three months too early under extremely dire circumstances. The doctors had ordered me to undergo all types of tests and lab work to try to determine what was still going on in my body. I was not allowed to eat or drink anything in preparation; that included I could not even brush my teeth that day. I also could not take a shower yet. The thought of not being able to brush my teeth or take a shower, absolutely sent me over an emotional edge and I remember crying uncontrollably. Timing would have it that my husband called with his daily check-in in the midst of my absolute meltdown. With grave concern mixed with terror in his voice thinking about his wife and tiny daughter, he said, "Babe.....what's wrong?" In between my still uncontrollable sobs I told my Protector, "They won't let me brush my teeth!"

This was one of my most vivid memories of realizing just how sick both Taryn and I were at that time. My body systems were out of control at the same time her tiny body was in the NICU clinging to life. While I was grateful for the ability to conceive and give birth under emergency circumstances, I also remembered reading the shocking childbirth statistics. According to the Centers for Disease Control and Prevention, approximately 700 women each year in the United States die as a result of pregnancy or delivery complications. Sadly, black mothers in the U.S. die at three to four times the rate of white mothers, one of the widest of all racial disparities in women's health.

During the nine postpartum days I spent in the hospital, as both Taryn and my lives felt like they hung in the balance of life or death, I remember confiding in God through prayer; "Please God.....if you just let us both live.....I will forever tell her story."

My Sister's Keyper

Glossary of Terms

Advocate/Advocacy – to speak or write in favor of; support or urge by argument; recommend publicly/ the act of pleading for, supporting, or recommending; active espousal or promotion.

Area of Eligibility – It means that under the law the IEP team has the flexibility to determine if a child qualifies for services. Criteria states that to qualify for special education services, a child must have one of the 13 disabilities as defined by IDEA and the impact of the disability must create a need for services.

1. Autism
2. Blindness
3. Deafness
4. Emotional Disturbance
5. Hearing Impairment
6. Intellectual Disability
7. Multiple Disabilities
8. Orthopedic Impairment
9. Other Health Impaired
10. Specific learning Disability
11. Speech/Language Impairment
12. Traumatic brain Injury
13. Visual Impairment)

Autism – a pervasive developmental disorder of children, characterized by impaired communication, excessive rigidity, and emotional detachment: now considered one of the autism spectrum disorders.

Cerebral Palsy – a form of paralysis believed to be caused by a prenatal brain defect or by brain injury during birth, most marked in certain motor areas and characterized by difficulty in control of the voluntary muscles.

Epilepsy – a disorder of the nervous system, characterized either by mild, episodic loss of attention or sleepiness (petit mal) or by severe convulsions with loss of consciousness (grand mal).

Exceptional Children – Children who deviate from the normal or average children in mental, physical and social characteristics to such an extent that they requires a modification of school practices or special educational services or supplementary instruction in other to develop to his maximum capacity

Guardian – A person who is entrusted by law with the care of the person or property, or both, of another, as a minor or someone legally incapable of managing his or her own affairs.

Guidepost – Anything serving as a guide; guideline.

IDEA – Individuals with Disabilities Education Act

Intellectual or Developmental Disability (IDD) – Includes many severe chronic conditions that are due to mental and/or physical impairments. IDD can begin at any time up to 22 years of age. It usually lasts throughout a person's lifetime.

Individual Education Plan (IEP) – This is a plan or program developed to ensure that a child with an identified disability who is attending an elementary or secondary educational institution receives specialized instruction and related services.

Letter of Intent – The goal of a letter of intent is to memorialize your knowledge of your child's needs so that you may guide future caregivers, guardians and trustees in providing the best possible care to your child

Multiple Handicap – Refers to simultaneous impairments (such as intellectual disability-blindness, intellectual disability-orthopedic impairment, etc.), the combination of which causes such severe educational needs that they cannot be accommodated in a special education program solely for one of the impairments.

Neonatal Intensive Care Unit (NICU) – stands for newborn intensive care unit. This is a nursery in a hospital that provides around-the-clock care to sick or premature babies. It has health care providers who have special training and equipment to give your baby the best possible care.

Occupational Therapy (OT) – Is a branch of health care that helps people of all ages who have physical, sensory, or cognitive problems. OT can help them regain independence in all areas of their lives.

Power-of-Attorney – A written document given by one person or party to another authorizing the latter to act for the former.

Premature Birth (Pre-Term) – A birth that takes place more than three weeks before the baby's estimated due date. In other words, a premature birth is one that occurs before the start of the 37th week of pregnancy. Premature babies, especially those born very early, often have complicated medical problems.

Parent Teacher Student Association (PTSA) – A volunteer association where parents, educators, students, and other citizens can be active in their schools and communities.

Self-Contained – Refers to a classroom, where a special education teacher is responsible for the instruction of all academic subjects. The classroom is typically separated from general education classrooms but within a neighborhood school.

Severe Pre-eclampsia – "a syndrome of high blood pressure (hypertension), fluid accumulation in the tissues and protein in the urine that becomes apparent in the second half of pregnancy."

Spinal Tap (Lumbar Puncture) – "a puncture into the subarachnoid space of the lumbar region to obtain spinal fluid for diagnostic or therapeutic purposes.

Vocational Rehabilitation – A process which enables persons with functional, psychological, developmental, cognitive, and emotional disabilities, impairments or health disabilities to overcome barriers to accessing, maintaining, or returning to employment or other useful occupations.

NOTES

NOTES

NOTES

NOTES

Notes

NOTES

Made in the USA
Columbia, SC
25 October 2020